Life in Victorian Ireland

DEIRDRE BROWN

RHONDA GLASGOW

Illustrations by
LYNNE HASTINGS

CONTENTS

THE
BLACKSTAFF PRESS

BELFAST

INTRODUCTION

Princess Victoria became Queen of the United Kingdom of Great Britain and Ireland in 1837 at the age of 18. In 1840 she married Albert, a German prince, and they had 4 sons and 5 daughters.

DID YOU KNOW?

The Christmas tree was a German tradition which was made popular by Prince Albert.

Queen Victoria died in 1901. For 64 years she had reigned over Great Britain and Ireland, and a large number of other countries ruled by Britain, known as the British Empire.

The Victorian Age was a time of great change which transformed people's lives.

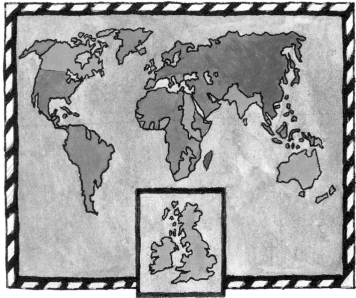

THE BRITISH EMPIRE, 1901
The countries shaded in pink were all ruled by Britain.

Prince Albert and Queen Victoria were very interested in the Great Exhibition of 1851. It was an international exhibition of industry and science held in London in a massive, specially built glasshouse called the Crystal Palace. It was hoped that all the wonderful exhibits would boost world trade.

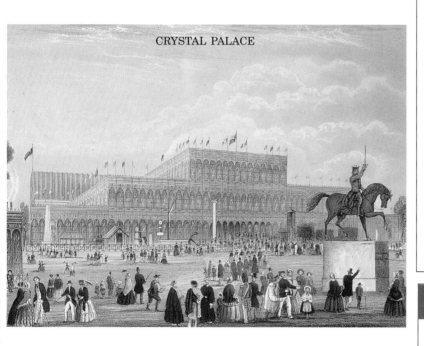

CRYSTAL PALACE

Two years later, in 1853, Victoria and Albert visited the great Irish Industrial Exhibition held in Dublin. Queen Victoria made 4 visits to Ireland. In 1849 she came to Belfast, her only visit to the north of Ireland.

INVENTIONS IN VICTORIAN TIMES

- electricity
- photography
- cinema
- telegraph
- telephone
- radio
- gramophone
- typewriter
- refrigerator
- ballpoint pen
- sewing machine
- washing machine
- motorcar
- motorcycle
- submarine
- steamship

THINK ABOUT

Is there any **evidence** of Victorian times in your home or near where you live?

Look for
- books
- buildings
- coins
- photographs
- paintings and drawings
- canals
- mills and factories
- ornaments
- schools
- railways
- statues and monuments

LIFE IN THE IRISH COUNTRYSIDE

In the early years of Victorian times most people in Ireland still lived in the countryside. The 1841 census tells us that only 14 per cent of the people lived in towns.

Most Irish land was owned by a very small number of extremely wealthy people – the **landlords**. Some landlords tried to improve their land and help the people, but many did not and spent little time on their estates, leaving their agents to manage their property and collect the rents.

The people who actually worked the land and paid the rents were called **tenants**. Some of these tenants, called **strong farmers**, rented a lot of land and were very prosperous, but most were much poorer, like the **small farmers** who rented only a few acres. The poorest of all were the **labourers,** who could not afford to rent any land, and they worked for the strong farmers and landlords.

LANDLORDS

A modern painting of
the Ward family in 1858

The Ward family of Castle Ward at Strangford, County Down, were typical of the landlord class. By the Victorian period they had owned this land for over 250 years and employed many people. More than 100 workers and house servants were hired to run the estate and look after the family when they were at home.

Edward Ward, 3rd Viscount Bangor, died in 1837, the year Princess Victoria was made Queen. His widow Lady Bangor lived at Castle Ward with their 6 sons. Soon after her husband's death she married Major Andrew Nugent, who was a widower with 2 daughters. They all lived together at Castle Ward, where the children were taught by a private tutor. When the boys were old enough they were sent to boarding school in England. Major Nugent made great improvements on the estate.

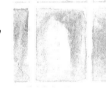

In County Down the Wards owned a total of 10,000 acres and the family's main income came from renting out their land and other properties.

The house at Castle Ward was surrounded by 1,000 acres of arable land, grazing and woodland, as well as formal gardens, parkland and an artificial lake. The estate had its own corn mill and saw mill, slaughterhouse, forge, laundry, dairy and lead mine.

Castle Ward estate, Strangford Lough, County Down, 1858 painted by Mary Ward

Castle Ward house, painted by Mary Ward

In 1850 the village of Audleystown, which lay on the edge of the Castle Ward estate, was cleared of its tenants and levelled to the ground so that Lady Bangor could have a better view of Strangford Lough. Major Nugent paid for the village people to emigrate to America, but some did not survive the long voyage from Strangford to Boston.

A modern painting of the stable yard at Castle Ward as it would have looked in the 1860s

STRONG FARMERS

The kitchen of a 'strong farmer'

Mary Carbery, who was the daughter of a strong farmer in County Limerick, gives us a good description of how her family lived in *The Farm by Lough Gur*:

1 My father, who was born in 1816, farmed about 200 acres of land, rented from Count de Salis. He gave constant employment to a number of men and women, some of whom lived in the four cottages on the farm. There was a potato garden for each cottage, also a goat. The men's wives and daughters helped with the milking of our fifty beautiful cows. Extra labourers, called "spalpeens", coming usually from Kerry and Cork, were hired for the potato digging in October.

Corradreenan farmhouse from County Fermanagh, reconstructed at the Ulster Folk and Transport Museum. The Elliott family which lived in this house farmed over 60 acres and was quite prosperous.

SMALL FARMERS

We know a lot about the condition of poor people in Ireland because a very thorough government inquiry into Irish poverty, called the Devon Commission, took evidence from many people in the 1840s. This is what John Connelly, a small farmer from County Monaghan, told the commissioners.

source

2 **How many acres of land do you hold?**
Three.

What family have you?
Seven children under the age of eighteen,
my wife and my mother.

Have you a cow?
Yes.

A pig?
Yes, a sow pig, and some young pigs.

Does the wife keep fowls?
Yes, only for that it would be very hard to pay the rent, only for
that and England. I go over every year to England to work.

How do you put together the money to pay the rent?
I put the wages I get in England and the fowls together,
and make up my rent with a great struggle.

What is your food?
Potatoes mostly, and sometimes a sup of milk.

Cruckaclady
farmhouse from
County Tyrone,
reconstructed at
the Ulster Folk
and Transport
Museum

Many small farmers lived
one-roomed or two-roomed hous

LABOURERS

Reconstruction of a labourer's house from Meenagarragh, County Tyrone, at the Ulster Folk and Transport Museum

Many farm labourers and their families lived in tiny one-roomed houses, with no windows and no chimneys.

Labourers also gave evidence of their living conditions to the Devon Commission, like Michael Sullivan from County Kerry.

3

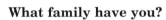

What quantity of ground do you hold?
I hold no ground. I am a poor man. I have nothing but my labour.

What family have you?
I have five children, under twelve years of age.

What is your general food for the family?
Nothing at all but dry potatoes.

Have you fish?
If my wife sells her eggs, or some thread she has spun, in the market, she may bring home with her a pennyworth or two of something to nourish the children for that night; but in general we never have meat or fish from one end of the year to the other, except what I may get at Christmas.

Have you generally milk with your potatoes?
Not a drop. I would think myself happy if I could give the five children milk.

Have you a pig?
Yes.

Where is he kept?
He must be kept in some part of the house, in a corner.

source

We have further evidence about how poor people in Ireland lived at this time; for instance, Gustave de Beaumont, a traveller from France, wrote:

source

'

4 Imagine four walls of dried mud, having for its roof a little straw or some sods, for its chimney a hole cut in the roof, or the door through which the smoke gets out. One single room contains father, mother, children and sometimes a grandfather or grandmother, there is no furniture in the wretched hovel; a single bed of straw serves the entire family. Five or six half-naked children may be seen crouched near a miserable fire, the ashes of which cover a few potatoes, the only food of the family. In the midst of all lies a dirty pig, the only thriving inhabitant of the place, for he lives in filth . . . I have just described the dwelling of the Irish agricultural labourer.

'

WRITE ABOUT

Using the written and pictorial information from this chapter, compare the lives of some of the people who lived in the countryside by copying out and filling in the grid below.

	NAME	DESCRIPTION OF HOME	SIZE OF FARM	PAYING OR RECEIVING RENT?
LANDLORD				
STRONG FARMER				
SMALL FARMER				
LABOURER				

THE GREAT FAMINE
1845–1850

The Famine 1848, Angela Antrim

COUNTDOWN TO DISASTER

In the 60 years between 1781 and 1841 the population of Ireland doubled from 4 million to 8 million. The greatest increase in population was in the very poorest class, the people who had no land or very little land. Many of these people survived by moving into mountainous or boggy country and growing just enough potatoes to keep themselves alive. When there were not enough potatoes, they had to beg or starve. In some areas the poor people were able to get work on the land of the bigger farmers. Sometimes they travelled to another part of Ireland or to England or Scotland to work on the harvest. They used the money they earned to pay their rent.

| GROWTH OF POPULATION IN IRELAND ||
YEAR	POPULATION
1731	3 MILLION
1781	4 MILLION
1821	7 MILLION
1841	8 MILLION

THE STORY OF THE FAMINE

What happened in Ireland in 1845?

When people went to harvest their potatoes in the autumn of 1845, they found the potatoes had been attacked by a fungus called blight which rotted the potatoes in the ground.

What did the people do?

They pawned anything they had, like clothing or furniture, and used the money to buy Indian meal, a variety of corn which the government brought in specially from America.

What happened the following year?

The potato harvest in 1846 was also attacked by blight. This time the people had nothing left. All their resources were gone. They faced starvation.

What could the starving people do?

They crowded into institutions called workhouses, hoping to be fed and given shelter in return for hard, unpaid work. The people hated the workhouses and only went there if they had no other choice. These bleak places soon filled up and could take no more.

What did the government do then?

The government set up public works – breaking stones, building roads and walls – so that people could earn the money to buy food.

Did the public works help?

People were already so weak from hunger and disease that they could not do much work. Because the price of food had risen and the wages were so low, the money they earned could buy very little.

What else was done to help the people?

The government set up soup kitchens to feed the hungry. Charitable people like the Quakers and some landlords also set up soup kitchens. By July 1847 half the population of Ireland was being fed daily at the soup kitchens.

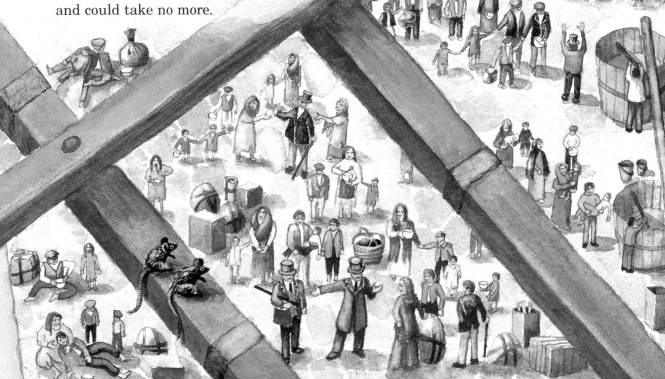

Did the soup kitchens prevent starvation?

Many people could not get near the soup kitchens and simply died where they lived. People who are weakened by hunger are easily infected by disease and many terrible diseases swept through Ireland. Disease also affected people who had not been starving. Many people like doctors, clergymen and charity workers, who worked among the poor, also died from fever.

Did all the landlords help their tenants?

Many landlords did not help. Some even made matters worse for their poorer tenants by evicting them from their homes when they could not pay the rent.

Emigrant ship leaving Belfast, 1852

What else did people do?

During these years many people left Ireland if they could afford to do so. Many went to Britain because it was possible to cross the Irish Sea for as little as a shilling. Many others emigrated to North America, Australia and New Zealand.

When did the Great Famine end?

In 1849 conditions were still very bad across much of Ireland. A cholera epidemic killed 36,000 people. By 1850 the worst was over but some areas were still badly affected by hunger and disease.

Over one million people died and one and a half million emigrated.

WHAT WAS SAID ABOUT STARVATION AND DISEASE

sources

5 'On 6 August 1846 – I shall not easily forget the day – I rode up as usual to my mountain property, and my feelings may be imagined when, before I saw the crop of potatoes, I smelt the terrible stench, now so well known as the death-sign of each field of potatoes.

W.S. TRENCH, LORD LANSDOWNE'S AGENT, DESCRIBING THE SECOND ATTACK OF POTATO BLIGHT'

6 'Some of the children were worn to skeletons, their features sharpened with hunger and their limbs wasted almost to the bone.

JOSEPH CROSSFIELD, A QUAKER, 1846

7 The workhouse contains a hundred more than it has room for . . . most of them were starving when they arrived. Their exhausted bodies were unable to digest the food given out to them and so they are dying in dozens.

Fermanagh Reporter, 1846

8 In Clifden, 5,000 are trying to live on seaweed. Around Westport nine-tenths of the people are in a state of starvation. In Roscommon and Tipperary people are eating horses and donkeys.

Saunder's Newsletter, 1847'

WHAT WAS SAID ABOUT STARVATION AND DISEASE

9 The state of the weather is making the misery of the poor worse. Among the thousands I meet I have not seen one who had clothing suitable for the bitter cold . . . what is seen is the very thin, pale, shivering and worn-out country people, wrapped in the most wretched of clothes, standing or crawling in the snow barefooted.

CHARITY WORKER IN MAYO, 1847

10 At first the townspeople of Cork were sympathetic to the Famine victims but when the fever began to spread they became alarmed for themselves and anxious to get rid of the wretched creatures. There was a house in a narrow alley that had been closed up for some days. We went in and saw 17 persons lying on the floor, all ill with fever. We got them to hospital but they all died.

FATHER MATHEW, CORK, 1847

11 The beginning of 1847 was marked by the spread of smallpox and dysentery among the poor, and several hundred cases of these diseases were transferred from the Workhouse to the General Hospital. Both sicknesses assumed a grave type, and dysentery was the worst form we ever witnessed.

DR ANDREW MALCOLM, BELFAST, 1851

sources

WHAT WAS SAID ABOUT GIVING HELP

sources

12 We had a relief meeting in Castlewellan, to be sure, but nothing was done. The landlords are absent when duty calls. There is no real sympathy among them for starving people.

A COUNTY DOWN MAN COMPLAINING ABOUT BAD LANDOWNERS; REPORTED IN *The Vindicator*, BELFAST,1846

13 We are comparatively well off in this neighbourhood, there is not want of food, but it is at such price, as to make it totally impossible for a poor man to support his family with the wages he receives. I do not exaggerate when I tell you that from the moment I open my hall door in the morning until dark, I have a crowd of women and children crying out for something to save them from starvation. I have been obliged to turn my kitchen into a Bakery and Soup shop . . . If there is no reduction in the price of food, hundreds will die of starvation.

GEORGE DAWSON, A GOOD LANDOWNER FROM CASTLEDAWSON, COUNTY DERRY, 1847

WHAT WAS SAID ABOUT EVICTION AND EMIGRATION

14 There were days in County Clare when I came back from some scenes of evicton so maddened by the sights of hunger and misery . . . that I felt disposed to take the gun from behind my door and shoot the first landlord I met.

CAPTAIN ARTHUR KENNEDY, POOR LAW INSPECTOR, KILRUSH, COUNTY CLARE, 1848

15 I shall not readily forget the scenes that occurred in Kenmare when I announced that Lord Lansdowne was prepared to send, at his own expense, to America anyone now in the workhouse who wanted to go. They thought at first that the news was too good to be true.

W.S. TRENCH, LORD LANSDOWNE'S AGENT, 1848

16 We beg your Majesty not to permit the helpless, the starving, the sick and the diseased, unfit as they are, to sail to these shores, which too many reach only to find a grave . . . We ask your Majesty's government to make sure that emigrant ships are large and airy, that enough space is given to the emigrants, and that a larger allowance of better food than is now available is provided on board.

AN ADDRESS FROM THE CANADIAN GOVERNMENT TO QUEEN VICTORIA AND HER GOVERNMENT, 1847

Emigration.
FOR PHILADELPHIA,
To Sail direct from Belfast on 5th MARCH,
The splendid New Philadelphia-built Ship,
SULTAN,
600 Tons Burthen—J. P. SAVAGE, Commander.
THIS splendid New Ship is Coppered and Copper-fastened, and has superior accommodations for Cabin, Second Cabin, and Steerage Passengers for the above Ship will be despatched punctually as find it to their advantage to go by this Ship, as they will save themselves both trouble and expense.
For Terms of Passage, apply to
SAMUEL McCREA,
General Emigration Office, 37, Waring-street, Belfast.
Belfast, February 5th, 1847.
(28)

WRITE ABOUT

Pretend you can go back in time and do some 'on the spot' reporting. You are a researcher for a television documentary about the Great Famine. Using 'The Story of the Famine' on pages 12–13 and the sources on pages 14–16, what can you find out under the following headings?

- WHAT CAUSED THE FAMINE?
- WHAT HAPPENED TO POOR PEOPLE?
- CLOTHING AND WEATHER
- DISEASE
- EVICTION
- THE LANDLORDS
- THE WORKHOUSES
- WHAT DID THE PEOPLE EAT?
- EMIGRATION

THINK ABOUT

Look back at the people you met in pages 5–9. They were Lady Bangor, Mary Carbery, John Connelly and Michael Sullivan. What do you think may have happened to each of them as a result of the Great Famine?

Who do you think may have
- survived?
- grown richer?
- died of hunger or disease?
- died in the workhouse?
- emigrated to Britain?
- emigrated to America?

Give reasons for your choices.

AFTER THE FAMINE

For many years after the Great Famine Irish people still relied heavily on the potato as their main source of food. Blight also remained a constant threat, causing lesser famines from time to time. It was not until the 1880s that a crop spray was invented that would kill the fungus.

Emigration continued steadily right through the century. Because the population was much smaller, there was more land to go round and people were not quite so poor as before. There were, however, many serious disturbances on the land in the late 19th century and the government decided to help Irish tenants, large and small, to buy out their farms. The day of the great landlords was over.

DID YOU KNOW?

In the 1930s the first blight-resistant potatoes were successfully bred by a man from County Antrim – John Clarke, who lived near Ballycastle.

EMIGRATION IN VICTORIAN TIMES

When the Great Famine ended, the population of Ireland had fallen drastically. As well as the one million who had not survived, there were one and a half million who had fled the country for a better life elsewhere. There was a great deal of **emigration** from European countries to the New World – North America, Australia and New Zealand. But the greatest emigration of all was from Ireland. Even before the Famine about 50,000 people had emigrated from Ireland every year and the numbers had rapidly increased during the Famine years. The Irish population continued to drop after the Famine. In the short space of sixty years it almost halved, from around eight million to four and a half million.

EMIGRATION FROM IRELAND 1845–1851	
1845	75,000
1846	105,000
1847	215,000
1848	180,000
1849	215,000
1850	210,000
1851	250,000

DECLINE IN IRISH POPULATION 1841–1901	
	million
1841	8.1
1851	6.6
1861	5.8
1871	5.4
1881	5.2
1891	4.7
1901	4.6

THE EMIGRANT'S JOURNEY

Most of the Irish who intended going to America travelled first to Liverpool or Glasgow, because the fares from these ports were cheaper than from Irish ports like Belfast, Derry and Cork. Many went to America via Canada because the fares were much cheaper on that route.

CROSSING THE ATLANTIC

Most of the emigrant ships were old wooden sailing ships which took about 4 weeks to make the voyage across the Atlantic Ocean. In very bad weather the journey could take 7 weeks. The ship supplied some basic food rations and a cook. There were no separate cabins for ordinary passengers. They had to sleep on narrow wooden bunks and supply their own bedding. Many passengers were already ill from famine fever, a kind of typhus.

The conditions on these ships were often appalling. Some ships were dangerously overcrowded, with not enough food and clean water to go round. These were called 'coffin ships' because many unfortunate people died of the fever, which spread rapidly among the passengers.

Famine fever was not the only danger that faced the emigrants. The crossing itself was dangerous and some ships sank in the Atlantic with heavy loss of life.

17 Report on the loss of an emigrant ship, *Belfast Commercial Chronicle*, 1847

The *Glasgow Herald* of Monday gives the fearful details of the loss of the emigrant ship *Exmouth*, from Londonderry to Quebec, on the coast of Islay, with the loss of upwards of *two hundred and forty lives!* Only three persons (sailors) escaped. All others – mostly women and young children – were drowned.

source

By the time the ships reached their destinations in Canada and America, the long journey and bad conditions had taken their toll. It has been estimated that over 5 per cent of emigrants sailing to Canada in 1848 died on board ship and another 25 per cent died on arrival.

source

This report was made by a doctor who inspected a ship when it arrived in Quebec in Canada.

18

"On boarding the boat I found the passengers in a terrible state of filth and disease. I found 26 cases of fever, and was told the names of 20 others, including the captain, who had died on the passage. The voyage had taken 72 days. I had to send 76 passengers to hospital, and 6 have died since landing . . .

The causes which have produced disease and death among these passengers are those so often stated by me in my annual reports: want of cleanliness and want of ventilation; lack of food and water, and that of a poor quality; overcrowding.

These causes produce fever, and once disease sets in, the stench from the bodies of the sick, dying and dead confined in the hold (the captain was kept below for 3 weeks on board after death) soon made the whole atmosphere unfit to breathe.

The passengers were not provided by the vessel with any food; their own stock was soon eaten. The vessel itself is 83 years old and not really fit for the voyage.

The number of passengers put on board exceeded by 60 or 70 the number allowed."

19 AN EMIGRATION SONG

THOUSANDS ARE SAILING
TO AMERICAY

Oh, you brave Irish people, wherever you be,
I pray stand a moment and listen to me.
Your sons and brave daughters are now going away,
And thousands are sailing to Americay.

Ah good luck to them now, and safe may they land,
They are pushing their way to a far distant strand,
For here in old Ireland no longer can stay,
And thousands are sailing to Americay . . .

THINK ABOUT

- What things were wrong with the emigrant ship described in the Quebec doctor's report? Make a list.
- Why did people who had crossed the Atlantic not write home to discourage their family and friends from making such a terrible journey?
- Did everyone who emigrated to the New World have a good life? Give reasons for your answer.
- Why do you think there are so many people of Irish descent living today in Glasgow and Liverpool?

THE LAND OF THE FREE?

For those who arrived safely, the New World held the promise of a better life. Andrew Greenlees, from near Larne in County Antrim, emigrated to New York in 1852. He was happy in America and did not regret leaving Ireland.

source

20 "This is a free country. Jack's as good as his master. If he don't like one of them, go to another. Plenty of work and plenty of wages, plenty to eat and no landlords. What more does a man want?"

Andrew Greenlees describing his job opportunities in America

DID YOU KNOW?

Of the 42 American presidents, 21 claim some degree of Irish descent, as do 3 Canadian prime ministers, 5 Australian prime ministers and 4 New Zealand prime ministers.

DID YOU KNOW?

The earliest settlers in Australia were convicts. In Victorian times some convicts were still being transported to Australia instead of being imprisoned in Britain. The last of these were transported in the late 1860s.

Not everyone was as fortunate as Andrew, however. Many of the poorer emigrants did not have time to prepare for their new lives so far from home and they arrived with no jobs to go to and very little money in their pockets.

Today, around 43 million Americans, 4 million Canadians, 4 million Australians and half a million New Zealanders claim Irish descent.

TALK ABOUT

Suppose you had lived on a farm in Victorian times and your eldest brother had emigrated to America. Which of the following statements might describe your feelings and opinions?

- I am sorry he has gone because I may never see him again.
- I hope he makes some money and sends it home to help us pay the rent.
- I hope he soon sends money for my ticket to America.
- Now that he's gone, I will inherit the farm.
- It's a good thing that so many are going to America because it means that those who are left have a better chance of work.

WRITE ABOUT

Compose a short letter which you think your brother in America might write to you and your family in Ireland. Write your reply.

THE WORKHOUSE

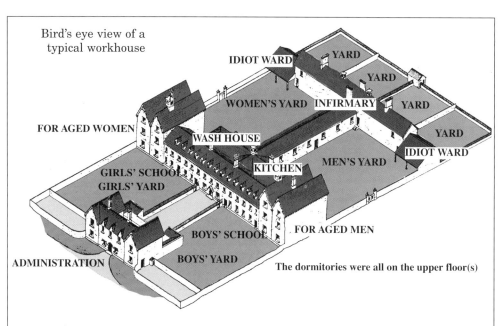

Bird's eye view of a typical workhouse

IDIOT WARD
YARD
YARD
WOMEN'S YARD
INFIRMARY
YARD
FOR AGED WOMEN
WASH HOUSE
YARD
KITCHEN
IDIOT WARD
MEN'S YARD
GIRLS' SCHOOL
GIRLS' YARD
BOYS' SCHOOL
FOR AGED MEN
ADMINISTRATION
BOYS' YARD

The dormitories were all on the upper floor(s)

In Victorian times there were large numbers of very poor people who survived by begging. The government thought that people were poor because they were lazy and it was decided to build **workhouses** which poor people would have to go into and where they would have to work in return for being clothed and fed.

These workhouses were made as unpleasant as possible to discourage people from crowding into them. Families were separated – husband from wife, child from parent – and discipline was very strict. Severe punishments were given to those who broke the rules. It was no wonder that all poor people hated the workhouse.

WRITE ABOUT

- Look at the bird's eye view of a workhouse. Write a short story about a child of your age whose family had to go there.

21 In this extract from *Sally Cavanagh*, a novel by Charles Kickham set in Ireland, a mother pleads to keep her children with her.

"The youngest little boy, sir!" exclaimed Sally Cavanagh, as she clasped her baby to her bosom . . . and looked imploringly into the face of the workhouse official. But it was no use; she must obey the rules. The children followed the official into a long corridor. Before the door closed behind them they turned round to take a last look at their mother, and as they did so their little hearts died within them.

Limavady workhouse, County Derry

THINK ABOUT

- The building in the photograph used to be a workhouse. Is there a building like this in your area? If so, what is it used for nowadays?

Source

THE WORKHOUSE DAY

The inmates of the workhouse were wakened at 6.00 a.m. After prayers and an inspection by the master, they had their miserable breakfast. They then worked in silence until supper. Women and girls did the household chores in the kitchen, the laundry and the hospital. Men and boys broke stones and picked oakum (unravelled the fibres in old hunks of rope). Then there were prayers and lights out at 9.00 p.m. in a cold, crowded dormitory. The children had an extra meal at lunchtime and 3 hours' schooling each day.

22 "Work for the able-bodied should be unpleasant and make them dislike the workhouse.
POOR LAW

Food must be worse than what is eaten by the poorest people.
POOR LAW"

OLIVER ASKS FOR MORE

23 "Oliver Twist and his companions suffered the tortures of slow starvation for three months . . . he was desperate with hunger and reckless with misery. He rose from the table, and advancing to the master, basin and spoon in hand, said: "Please Sir, I want some more." The master aimed a blow at Oliver's head with the ladle; pinioned him in his arms and shouted for the beadle. Oliver was ordered into solitary confinement in a dark room for a week and a bill [notice] was pasted on the gate offering £5 reward to anyone who would take Oliver Twist off the hands of the parish by giving him an apprenticeship."

from *Oliver Twist* by CHARLES DICKENS

Workhouses were not phased out until after the First World War (1914–1918), when some became hospitals.

TALK ABOUT

True or False?

Discuss the following statements in your group and decide whether they are True or False.

- Workhouses were like holiday camps.
- Life in the workhouse was very hard.
- People hated the workhouse.
- Poor people were lazy.
- People would have done almost anything to avoid having to go to the workhouse.
- People only went to the workhouse if they were starving.
- The workhouse was like being put in prison without having committed a crime.

THINK ABOUT

Evaluating the evidence

- Do you think that the evidence in novels like *Sally Cavanagh* and *Oliver Twist* or the musical *Oliver* is reliable? Give reasons for your answer.

LIFE IN IRISH TOWNS

One of the great changes which occurred in Victorian times was that large numbers of people left the countryside and went to work in mills and factories in industrial towns.

There were many of these industrial towns in England but not many in Ireland. The biggest industrial town in Ireland was Belfast, which became the fastest-growing city in the British Isles in the 19th century.

Most of the people who crowded into Victorian towns were poor people escaping from hunger in the countryside. There was also a growing number of middle-class people whose families had become wealthy through industry and trade. Although these people were not as grand as the country landowners, some of them grew very rich. Other people who grew prosperous in Victorian times were professional people like doctors and lawyers and some of the larger shopkeepers. In Belfast some of the richest people had made their money out of the linen industry, like the Charley family of Dunmurry.

GROWTH OF POPULATION IN BELFAST	
YEAR	POPULATION
1831	53,000
1851	87,000
1871	174,000
1891	226,000
1901	350,000

The Mayne family relaxing in their Belfast home in the 1860s. The Maynes owned a large bookshop in the centre of the city.

Letitia Charley, born in 1831, describes her pleasant home:

24

"It was a roomy, airy, sunny house, not large enough to have spare rooms, but with a place for everything and everybody. Our kitchens were cheerful and airy and had large wooden presses to hold stores of all kinds.

Our parents, our sisters and the boys all slept in rooms off the landing. The older girls also had a nice little sitting room of their own here, filled with favourite books and drawings, and there was a piano where Cecilia played and sang while Caroline played old Irish airs on the harp.

Up another flight of stairs was our nursery where we could romp and play to our hearts' content."

source

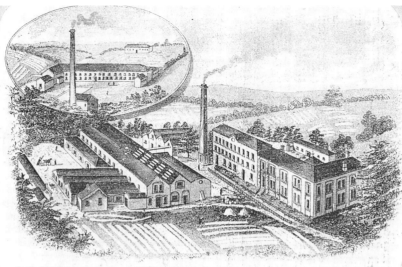

J. & W. CHARLEY & C⁰ˢ WORKS. DUNMURRY. Nᴿ BELFAST

Charley's linen mill, Dunmurry

Unlike their wealthy **employers**, the vast majority of workers lived in misery and squalor. The large numbers of **working-class** poor who crowded into mill towns were forced to work long, hard hours and lived in small, cramped houses which were damp and stuffy. These houses did not have flush toilets and running water like today. Instead, street water pumps provided a supply of water which was very often contaminated by waste and manure leaking into the water pipes.

These miserable living conditions caused terrible diseases which killed a great many people. **Typhoid** was carried in dirty food and water; **typhus** was carried by lice and fleas; **tuberculosis** was caused by overcrowding and lack of ventilation. **Cholera** was also carried in food and water, and outbreaks of cholera would sometimes spread out of control. All these diseases were highly contagious. In the cholera epidemic of 1848–1849 over 1,000 people died in Belfast.

In 1900 the poorest people still lived in old houses built around a court, like this one near Smithfield in Belfast. Most working people, however, lived in newer houses which had their own yards.

25 In the 1840s Dr Andrew Malcolm wrote detailed descriptions of how the poor lived in Belfast. He realised there was a link between housing and health.

'With few exceptions, the houses are built in a wretched manner, a large number of them consist of double rows clapt together [back to back], the result of which is that the people who lived in them, having no proper drains or sewers, have to throw their slops, refuse, etc., in front of the door . . . The whole surface of this neighbourhood is constantly kept in a filthy and most awful state, covered thickly over with heaps of manure and every kind of rubbish . . . which, when rain falls, sinks into the earth, finding its way into the water supply.'

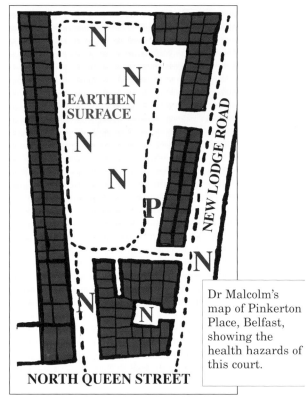

Dr Malcolm's map of Pinkerton Place, Belfast, showing the health hazards of this court.

N = nuisance (manure heap)
P = pump
■ = back to back houses
– – – = open sewers

THINK ABOUT

• Look at the map and read the source. What were the dangers to people's health described by Dr Andrew Malcolm? Make a list.

• What would have been needed to improve these conditions?

• In Victorian times death rates were much higher in towns than in the country. Why do you think this was so?

DID YOU KNOW?

In 1861 Prince Albert died of typhoid when he was 42, probably because of defective drains at Windsor Castle. The Albert Memorial clock in Belfast was built in his memory in 1867.

In Victorian times the average age at death was much lower than today and few people could expect to live beyond their forties. Many mothers died giving birth to their children, many children died as infants and many more died before they reached adulthood. Health care was not provided by the government and the majority of people could not afford to pay for doctors. Those who could afford to pay for medical treatment were not always cured of their

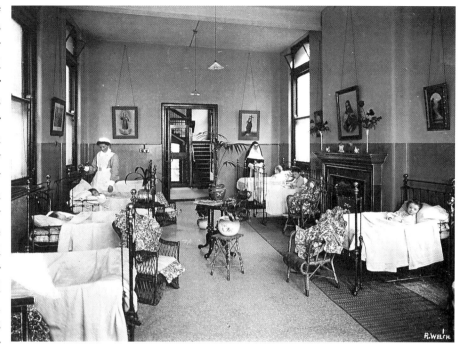

illness, particularly if it was a serious one. Hospitals were full of germs and often made sick patients even worse. During this period, however, some improvements were made when doctors and nurses became aware of the importance of hygiene. The greatest improvement of all came as a result of a cleaner water supply and better drainage systems which reduced disease.

Children's ward, Mater Hospital, Belfast, around 1900. By that time hygiene had become very important in hospitals.

MEDICAL ADVANCES IN VICTORIAN TIMES

- James Simpson uses chloroform as an anaesthetic.

- Louis Pasteur discovers link between bacteria and disease.

- Joseph Lister uses antiseptic spray in surgery.

- Florence Nightingale's nursing methods revolutionise hospital care.

- X-rays used for the first time in 1895.

- Vaccination and immunisation methods are developed.

SIXTEEN YEARS A MAIDEN
ONE TWELVEMONTH A WIFE
ONE HALF HOUR A MOTHER
THEN I LOST MY LIFE

ERECTED BY JOHN REID
IN MEMORY OF HIS FIVE CHILDREN
WHO DIED IN INFANCY.
ALSO HENRIETTA REID WHO DIED
5TH AUGUST 1841 AGED SIX YEARS.
ALSO HIS DAUGHTER SOPHIA REID
WHO DIED 1ST JANUARY 1842
AGED 15 YEARS.
ALSO HIS SON JOHN REID.

CHILDREN AT WORK

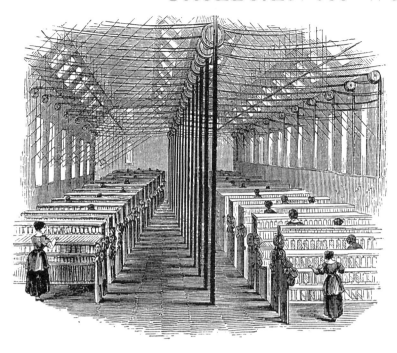

Belfast mill, 1830s

Throughout Queen Victoria's reign children from poor families received little or no schooling, but were made to work to earn desperately needed money. In towns it was sometimes only children and women who could find work in the factories because employers paid them less than men and so preferred to hire them. Before the industrial age, it had always been taken for granted that children would do their share of the family's work as soon as they were old enough. However, in the 19th century their lives worsened and many children from a very young age had to work up to 12 hours a day in terrible conditions and with dangerous machines which had no safety guards to prevent accidents. By the time their long day was over they were filthy and exhausted.

Some people were concerned about the awful working conditions in factories and mines. In 1833, a few years before Victoria became Queen, the government set up a Commission of Inquiry to investigate just how bad the conditions were. Here is some of the evidence the commissioners collected from children working in Belfast cotton and linen mills.

Mill girls in Belfast, 1830s

source 26

Catherine Macaulay, ten years old. Says that she has worked for two years in the spinning-room, and is greatly troubled with a pain in her head, which she never had before she came into the mill. Says she cannot write.

source 27

Sarah Pollock, aged twelve. Can't say that she is very tired, but she would like to have a shorter time to work, even if she were to get less wages for it. Two or three slaps on the side of the head is the most she ever got, when she has been late with her share (of the bobbins). Can read. Has never written since she left the day-school four years ago. She usually gets up at four o'clock. She is glad that she has been sent to the mill, for "she earns her mother money".

source 28

Marcella Robinson, aged eleven. Likes it very well. Was never tired when they worked twelve hours. Nobody has beat her since she came, and she never saw any other little girl beat. Can read a little; can't write. It is too late when the mill stops to go to an evening school . . . When they were working twelve hours, she earned 2s. [10p] per week; and now, when they work only eight hours, she gets 1s. 2d. [6p]. She would sooner be working twelve hours.

source 29

Robert Laird, aged fourteen. Doesn't like the mill very much. Doesn't think it is a very wholesome place. The place is very stuffy, and there is such a deal of fluff and dust flying through it. Sometimes has got a clout from his master; nothing more than that. Can read; can't write. Goes to the evening school generally.

WRITE ABOUT

Copy out the grid and summarise the evidence to be found in these sources.

	Catherine	Sarah	Marcella	Robert
Age at present?				
Do they enjoy their work?				
Have they been beaten?				
Do they go to school?				
Can they read?				
Can they write?				
Do they want to work longer hours?				

Is there anything about the evidence of these children which surprises you?

There were a few factory owners who cared about their workers and who built, on country sites, model factories and model villages which provided schools and good housing. This was very rare, however, and most workers were employed by rich manufacturers who were only interested in keeping their machines operating around the clock at as low a cost as possible.

Government reports, and **campaigns** by people like Lord Shaftesbury who were concerned about the effects upon children of long hours of work and no schooling, resulted in changes being made. These **reforms** were put in place throughout the rest of the century and working conditions for men, women and children gradually improved.

Lord Shaftesbury,
1801–1885

In the 1840s laws were passed which said that children under 9 years of age were not allowed to work for more than 6 hours a day, and they were to have 3 hours a day at school. These children were called **half-timers**.

HALF-TIMERS

Half-timers had to obtain a Certificate of Attendance. If their attendance at school was irregular they were not allowed to work the following week. Sometimes these children had not been to school at all until they began to work in the mill, and they were on average about 4 years behind children who had been lucky enough to attend school full time.

Half-timers were often separated from the other pupils not just because they were behind in reading and writing but because of the smell they brought with them from the mill.

source

The 1870 Powis Report on education describes the day-to-day existence of half-timers.

30 "Where half-time children are employed there are two sets of them working the day but it is the morning set only to which I shall refer. Many of them living a few hundred yards away from the mill, must rise during all states of the weather, both winter and summer, at 5.45 a.m. at the latest to be at the mill and at work at 6.00 a.m. They then work until breakfast time at 8.15 a.m, go home to breakfast (probably bread and tea), return at 8.45 a.m. and work till 12 noon in a moist and heated atmosphere . . . At 12 they are permitted to go home to "take a piece", that is, a morsel of treacle and bread, or dry bread in their hands, eating it as they hurry to school, where they remain till 3 and then go home to dinner, that is, potatoes and buttermilk when they can get it, often prepared for them by a child younger than themselves because the mother is working in the factory, or dry bread again."

source

The Powis Report also tells us what half-timers looked like.

31 "The afternoon set come to school in a state of personal dirt and squalor, which makes mixing with them very unpleasant. The room is filled with the stink of the flax oil; the children's faces are smeared with the oil and dust which sticks to their fingers after their work; their scanty ragged clothing, with an old shawl thrown over their shoulders to protect them from the rain, makes them look different from the other children who dislike them."

WRITE ABOUT

- Using these extracts from the Powis Report, make a timetable of the half-timer's day.

- Imagine that you are one of the children in the school who did **not** work in the mill. Describe one of the half-timers who arrives from work at midday and say how you feel about him or her joining your class.

The improvements in working conditions came about very slowly. Government inspectors were given the job of checking that factory owners obeyed the new laws. It was not until 1901 that children under 12 were not allowed by law to work for a living.

STREET TRADERS

Not all town children found work in the factories and mills and many had to work in the streets. We can find out about the many kinds of jobs they did from sources like newspapers and government reports.

An orphan flower-seller, aged 11

source

Here are some extracts from a government report on street trading in Belfast in 1908, shortly after Victoria's reign ended.

32

'We estimate that there are between 300 and 400 children selling papers every morning on the streets of Belfast. A few sell laces and matches. There are about 50 or 60 girls in Belfast engaged largely as flower sellers. A lot of boys are engaged in hawking sticks. Other boys are employed by merchants to deliver messages, some sell laces and studs. Some of these children do not attend school at all, but work from 8 o'clock in the morning until 10 o'clock at night.

The paper sellers annoy the public so much by shouting and wrestling and they have a system of jostling people in the streets to sell their papers: they jump into tramcars, and are a very great nuisance about restaurants, hotels, clubs and places of public resort. They get into the doorways of offices, and will hardly move out, even for the owners.

I have seen these poor little things, especially on Saturday evenings, out very very late, and they with hardly enough clothing to cover their nakedness. Many of the deaths from consumption [tuberculosis] are among children who are out in all weathers.

What do they do with their earnings? They hand them over to their parents.'

DID YOU KNOW?

Dr Thomas John Barnardo from Dublin was so concerned about the plight of destitute children that he founded the first of his famous homes in east London in 1870. By 1900, 8,000 children were in his care.

A match girl, aged 8

Crossing sweepers, like these boys aged 8 and 10, cleared away the horse manure that covered Victorian streets.

DOMESTIC SERVANTS

In Victorian times, most upper-class and middle-class people kept servants. Wealthy households like the one at Castle Ward had lots of servants to do different jobs but less wealthy households would sometimes employ just one girl to do everything – the **maid-of-all-work**.

Mrs Isabella Beeton (1836–1865) was regarded as an expert on cookery and house management. Victorians were very influenced by her books, from which we can get a good idea of the kind of work servants had to do. These are the chores that Molly, a maid, had to do before breakfast.

source

33 ' The general servant, or maid-of-all-work, deserves our pity. Her life is a solitary one, and in some places her work is never done. She has to rise with the lark, for she has to do in her own person all the work which in larger houses is performed by cook, kitchen-maid, and housemaid.

Mrs Beeton, 1860 '

MOLLY'S MORNING

source

34 ' My duties begin by opening the shutters of all the lower rooms in the house; I then brush up the kitchen-range, light the fire, clear away the ashes, clean the hearth, and polish with a leather the bright parts of the range. I need to be as quick as I can. After putting on the kettle, I then go to the dining-room to get it in order for breakfast. I first roll up the rug, take up the fender, shake and fold up the tablecloth, then sweep the room, carrying the dirt towards the fireplace; I then lay a coarse cloth over the carpet and I clean the grate. When the grate is finished, the ashes cleared away, the hearth cleaned, and the fender put back in its place, I have to dust the furniture, and if there are any ornaments or things on the sideboard, I must not dust round them, but lift them out on to another place, dust well where they have been standing, and then replace the things. After the rug is put down, the tablecloth arranged, and everything in order, I lay the cloth for breakfast, and then shut the dining-room door.

The hall must now be swept, the mats shaken, the door-step cleaned, and any brass knockers or handles polished up with the leather. The family's boots must now be cleaned. I then have to wash my hands and face, put on a clean white apron, and be ready for my mistress when she comes downstairs.

Then I carry the urn into the dining-room, where my mistress will make the tea or coffee, and sometimes will boil the eggs. In the meantime I cook the bacon, kidneys, fish, etc . . .

adapted from Mrs Beeton's *Book of Household Management*

Going into **domestic service**, as this type of work was called, often led to a life of drudgery. Servants had to live in the homes of their employers, so that they would be there to do work at any time of the day or night. Their wages were very low and they had very little time off.

WRITE ABOUT

- Count the number of chores which Molly had to do before breakfast.
- At what time do you think she had to get up?
- Compare Molly's work with what needs to be done in a modern house.
- If you had been the child of very poor parents in Belfast in Victorian times, would you rather have worked in a mill or been a servant? Give reasons for your choice.

Some poor country people who had many children were not able to feed them all, so as soon as the children were about 8 or 9 years old, they were sent to the **hiring fair** in the hope that they would get a live-in job with a farmer. If they were hired at the fair, they had to agree to stay with the farmer for 6 months. Hiring fairs were held in market towns, usually in May and November. Men and women were hired as well as children.

HIRED FARM SERVANTS

Paddy Gallagher from Donegal was sent to the Strabane hiring fair in the 1880s. This is what he remembers about that time.

35 When I was ten years of age I could not wait. My father had not enough money to pay the rent and the shop's debts. It was the same with the neighbours. A crowd of us boys were got ready for the hiring fair at Strabane.

I'll always mind the morning I first left home. I think I see my mother as she handed me my four shillings for the journey. She was crying. She kissed me again and again . . . We were all barefooted; we had our boots in our bundles . . .

When we reached Strabane we all huddled together, until the farmers made us walk up and down to see how we were set up and judge what mettle was in us. Anybody who looked tired or faulty in any way was passed over. The strong boys were picked up quickly and I was getting scared I would be left . . .

Then a farmer came up to me and made me walk up and down. "How much do you want for six months?" he said. I said, "Three pounds ten." I heard him whispering to another fellow, "He is wee, but the neck is good", and he then offered me two pounds ten.

The other man caught both our hands in his, hit our hands a slap, and said, "Bought and sold for three pounds." We both agreed.

source

Children who were hired by farmers would have fed the animals, milked the cows, helped with the churning of butter, lifted stones from the fields, planted seeds and set potatoes, weeded and hoed, picked potatoes, tied and stacked sheaves of corn, cut turf and made hay. They would have herded animals and dug and pulped turnips for animal feed. Girls would also have done household chores. Some children had good living quarters and ate with the family; others slept in draughty barns or attics and were fed the same food as the animals.

For many boys and girls their 6 months' work with a farmer was a time of loneliness and long hours of hard, heavy labour but some people had happy memories of being hired.

WRITE ABOUT

- Why did Paddy and his friends have to leave their homes in Donegal and go to the hiring fair at Strabane?
- Why do you think the children were keen to go to be hired?
- What phrase in Paddy's account shows us that farmers chose a child to be hired in much the same way as they would have chosen an animal at the fair?
- Why did farmers in Victorian times need a lot more farm workers than they do today?
- Pretend you have to go a hiring fair. Make up a short drama about it.

source

This is how one old man looked back.

36 " I have never regretted having come to the employment of this farmer. He was an honest, hardworking man who readily appreciated a boy who was interested in farming and willing to work. I took great pride in the knowledge I acquired at this farm. "

TALK ABOUT

- Look back over the different kinds of work children had to do in Victorian times. Imagine a conversation between Catherine, the mill girl, Molly, the house maid, and Paddy, the farm worker. What would they say about each other's work?

Ballymoney hiring fair, around 1900

CHILDREN AT SCHOOL

Moy
National School,
County Tyrone,
around 1890

In the early 19th century most children did not go to school. Their parents could not afford the school fees or the cost of books and they needed the children to help with the farm work or make some money by working in the mill.

In 1831 in Ireland the government decided to set up a system of National Schools. It wanted children to learn the 3 Rs – Reading, wRiting and aRithmetic – and it wanted all Protestant and Catholic children to learn together.

Even though National Schools were quickly set up throughout the country, many less fortunate children were still unable to go to school. The system was not completely free and children did not have to attend school as they do today.

Ballyveridagh
National School,
County Antrim,
reconstructed at
the Ulster Folk
and Transport
Museum

Parents were expected to make small payments for books, according to what they could afford, and they sent turf, coal or money for fuel for the fire. Most of these children probably went to school at about 5 or 6 years of age and left at about 12 or 13. The length of the school day varied from place to place and from season to season and holidays were not as long as they are today.

- Compare the photograph of Moy National School on page 36 with your own classroom. Discuss how being a pupil there might have been different from being a pupil in your school.

- Look at these items which were used in National Schools. Do we still use these today? If not, why not?

Ink bottle, pen and copy book

School clock and abacus

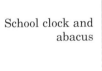

Tonic solfa chart for singing lessons

Bell, slate and school rules

TEACHERS

source

In *Roses and Rainbows*, Florence Mary McDowell describes a typical Victorian schoolmaster.

37 'The Master was a hard man. He drove everyone with little mercy. He drove himself with even less. His mainsprings of interest were his interpretation of Christ Crucified and his genuine love of music. To Mary he often showed kindness. Yet he found no difficulty in reconciling the love of God with soaking a bucketful of canes in cold water on Friday, ready for the slaughter of the innocents, dirty or stupid or both, on the coming Monday.

Swish! Swish! Swish! went the wet canes on trembling bony fingers thrust out with pale-faced bravado.'

source

38 'Our wee school's a great wee school,
It's built of bricks and plaster,
The only thing that's wrong with it
Is our wee baldy master.

He goes to the pub on Saturday night,
He goes to church on Sunday,
He prays the Lord to give him strength
To slaughter us on Monday.'

TRADITIONAL RHYME

source

39

Not all teachers were cruel to their pupils. Robert Grange attended Ballyclare National School and he remembers the kindness of his master.

'In the cold, frosty days of winter he always kept a large metal pot filled to the brim with delicious soup, made by himself, simmering on the peat fire, and at regular intervals during the day a generous helping was ladled into the bowls, which together with a supply of big bone spoons, he himself provided for each child. '

THINK ABOUT

- Why do you think Victorian teachers often used the cane?
- Why do you think Robert Grange's teacher made soup for his pupils?
- Re-enact a Victorian school day in your own classroom or in one of the National Schools in the Ulster Folk and Transport Museum. You could dress in suitable clothing; set the desks in rows; use the rote method to recite a poem or learn tables; write on slates or try nibbed pens and ink, and experience a very strict teacher wielding a cane! What could you bring for lunch?

DID YOU KNOW?

Vere Foster, who lived in Belfast, was a Victorian who devoted his large fortune to the improvement of education in Ireland. His handwriting copybooks of Victorian sayings like 'spare the rod and spoil the child' became world famous.

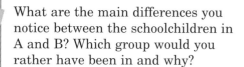

WRITE ABOUT

What are the main differences you notice between the schoolchildren in A and B? Which group would you rather have been in and why?

A

B

CHILDREN AT PLAY

In Victorian times children did not have as much choice as children today in deciding what to do in their leisure time. Many children had to work so hard that they had little time or energy left for play, and there was often no money to spare for toys and trips. Children from wealthier families had a better life and enjoyed playing with the popular toys that were in fashion during that time. But even a child from a rich family would not have had as many toys as the average child today.

These little girls are playing 'wee shop'. What tells you that they are probably quite poor children? Did you play shop when you were small?

'Churchie one over' was a rather rough game mainly played by boys.

Circuses, variety concerts and the music hall were all very popular in Victorian times. Touring companies performed in theatres like the New Grand Opera House and Cirque, which opened in Belfast in 1895.

TALK ABOUT

- Discuss why some of your favourite activities today would not have been possible in Victorian times.

Sea-bathing became a very popular Victorian pastime. Ladies would have changed in huts like these at Portstewart, County Derry. They then would have been pulled a little way into the water by donkeys. Why do you think this was done?

TRANSPORT IN VICTORIAN TIMES

THE STEAM ENGINE

The invention of the steam engine changed the world. People who had for generations worked in their own homes and farms and sold their goods in markets went to live in towns to work in steam-powered mills and factories. The products manufactured in these mills were much cheaper than the old hand-made articles. Travel between towns became much faster and more reliable. Travel across the seas took a lot less time and became much safer. All kinds of goods from different parts of the British Isles and from distant areas of the world became available to people in Ireland.

THE RAILWAYS

The greatest change in land transport was the invention of the steam locomotive. For the first time in the history of the world, mechanical power instead of animal power was used in land transport. Before that, horse-drawn barges navigated the canals which had been built in the 18th century and horse-drawn carriages travelled the old coach roads.

Whitehead,
County Antrim, 1862

The railways came to Ireland in the 1830s just around the time that Queen Victoria came to the throne. The Dublin & Kingstown Railway, built by William Dargan, opened in 1834 and the Ulster Railway between Belfast and Lisburn opened in 1839. Some people were against the railways and not everyone wanted to travel by train. Nevertheless, railways spread quickly all over Britain and Ireland.

> **'** N**o** locomotive could travel at 10 m.p.h., but if it does, I will undertake to eat a stewed engine wheel for breakfast! **'**
>
> **40**

A

B

C

WRITE ABOUT

- Why do you think some people were against the railways?
- There were 3 different classes of carriage. Look at the pictures A, B and C, and say which ones illustrate 1st class, 2nd class and 3rd class. Why do you think so?
- How did the railways change people's lives?
- Where is the nearest railway to you?

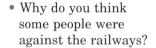

IRISH RAILWAYS IN 1899
This map shows how railways had spread across Ireland by the end of th 19th century.

By 1900 over 3,000 miles of track had been laid in a network throughout the country and most people did not have to travel far to get to a railway line.

The railways made huge changes to people's lives. They quickly delivered all kinds of goods, including the mail and newspapers, all over the country. They made it possible for well-off people to move out of the cities and travel each day to work. People could now travel easily to the new seaside resorts and go on outings like Sunday school excursions.

Waiting for the Bangor train at Queen's Quay Station, Belfast

SHIPS AND SHIPBUILDING

Around 1800 the steam engine was being tried out on sea as well as on land. By 1820 there were regular steamboat services on the short sea route between Ireland and Great Britain. As steam engines became more powerful, steamships were able to make longer journeys. The first transatlantic journey was made by the *Sirius*, a wooden paddle steamer which made the voyage from Cobh, County Cork, to New York in 1838. The first **iron** steamship to cross the Atlantic was the *Great Britain* in 1845. It was built by Brunel, the famous English engineer and inventor.

The *Oceanic* was built in Belfast by Harland and Wolff. This liner was launched in 1870 and was powered by both sail and steam.

THINK ABOUT

• Unlike sailing ships, steamships had to carry coal for fuel. What problems do you think this posed for shipping companies?

By the end of Queen Victoria's reign most of the ships in the world were steamships and they carried British goods, including Irish linen, all over the world. These ships also brought to the United Kingdom wheat from North America, beef from Argentina, lamb from New Zealand and fruit from many tropical countries.

By 1900 the greatest builder of **steel** ships in the world was the Belfast firm of Harland and Wolff. It employed thousands of workers and had helped to make Belfast a prosperous city. At the beginning of the new century Belfast was the third busiest port in the United Kingdom.

HORSE-DRAWN VEHICLES

In Victorian times nearly all road vehicles were pulled by horses and, at first, only well-off people could afford to use them. There were hackney cabs which could be hired like taxis today, but most of the vehicles for hiring in Ireland were jaunting cars.

WRITE ABOUT

- Why were trams cheaper to run than omnibuses?
- What would the drawbacks have been of all this horse-drawn traffic?

Horse-drawn omnibuses appeared in Belfast from the early 1860s, allowing people who could afford the fares to move out of the city centre. In the 1870s horse trams running on iron rails in the road became more popular. Horses found it easier to pull these trams than the omnibuses, fewer horses were needed, and so fares came down because they were cheaper to run.

Horse-drawn carriage

Many wealthy people had their own carriages. Extremely wealthy people kept several carriages as well as a lot of horses to pull the carriages and to use for riding. They also needed to employ coachmen to drive the carriages and grooms to look after the horses. Horse-drawn vehicles were also used to carry goods from the docks and the railway stations to the shops.

Horses were expensive to keep and to feed and people tried to find other ways of pulling vehicles. Steam buses and steam cars were tried but they were noisy and heavy and a law was passed in 1865 (the Red Flag Act) saying that they were restricted to 4 m.p.h. in towns and that a man waving a red flag had to walk in front of them.

Horse-drawn tram in Belfast around 1900

There was a breakthrough in 1885 when two Germans, Karl Benz and Gottlieb Daimler, each came up with a solution – fitting the new internal combustion engine to a lightweight carriage. This resulted in the **horseless carriage** (later called the motorcar). The first motorcar in Ireland was a Benz in 1896.

DID YOU KNOW?

The first hydro-electric tramway in the world was designed and built by William Traill from County Antrim. It began to operate in 1883 between Portrush and Bushmills, and was extended to the Giant's Causeway in 1887.

THE BICYCLE

The bicycle was developed in Victorian times. One of the most extraordinary Victorian bicycles was the **Big Wheeler**, or **Penny Farthing**. Before chain drive and gears were invented the only way to make bicycles go faster was to make the wheel with the pedals bigger and bigger. The average diameter of a Penny Farthing wheel was 137 centimetres (54 inches). These bicycles were great fun for fit young men but too dangerous for anybody else. Victorian women, in their long dresses, could not have ridden these bicycles.

By 1890 the development of gears and chain drive allowed bicycles with small wheels to perform just as well as those with big wheels. Smaller wheels allowed riders to sit on the saddle and touch the ground with their feet, and so it was called the **safety bicycle**. These small wheels, however, gave a bumpy ride on rough roads.

Lady riding a safety bicycle

THINK ABOUT

- Why do you think Big Wheelers were called Penny Farthings?

- How tall are you? Could you have ridden a Penny Farthing?

Early bicycles had wooden wheels with metal rims, which also made them very uncomfortable to ride. The first really comfortable wheel was only created after the invention of the **pneumatic tyre,** made of rubber and filled with air. It was invented by John Boyd Dunlop, a Scot who had a veterinary practice in Belfast.

The combination of the safety bicycle and the pneumatic tyre meant that hundreds of thousands of people bought bicycles. Many who could not afford a horse now had their own form of personal transport. Women in particular welcomed the new safety bicycle. It is still used by millions of people all over the world.

DID YOU KNOW?

In 1885 Gottlieb Daimler fitted a petrol engine to his bicycle to invent the first motorcycle.

GETTING ABOUT IN VICTORIAN
TOWNS AND CITIES

This picture of Donegall Place in the centre of Belfast is an 1889 advertisement for the newly opened department store of Robinson & Cleaver. This large store had electric light and a beautiful marble staircase and was a favourite shopping place until it closed down in 1984 and was converted into other smaller shops.

The advertisement gives us a lot of information on the different forms of transport Victorian people used and also gives us a good idea of how Victorian people dressed.

WRITE ABOUT

Look at the picture:

- How many times can you see the name Robinson & Cleaver? Why do you think the name appears so often?

- Why do you think there are no poor people in the picture? What kind of people would an advertiser want to show using a department store?

- Do you think this picture is as accurate as a photograph? Give reasons for your answer.

- How many of the following forms of transport can you spot? Bicycle, horseback, phaeton (open carriage), tricycle, horse tram, jaunting car, closed carriage, horse-drawn delivery van.

- Note that everyone is wearing headgear. Pick a man and a woman and make drawings of them, showing as clearly as you can the clothes they are wearing.

- Find some children and describe what they are wearing.

TALK ABOUT

Looking at this scene today, how has transport changed since Victorian times?

IRISH VICTORIAN INVENTIONS AND DISCOVERIES

Many Victorian inventions and discoveries were made by Irish people. Here are a few examples – can you find any more?

The first practical system of colour photography was invented in 1894 by John Joly from County Offaly.

John Philip Holland from County Clare launched the first successful submarine in New York City in 1881. Holland's submarines were later ordered by the United States Navy.

The first successful transatlantic cable, from Ireland to Canada, was laid in 1866 by master navigator Captain Robert Charles Halpin from Wicklow, using instruments designed by Lord Kelvin who was born in Belfast.

The 3rd Earl of Rosse's telescope *Leviathan* at Birr Castle, County Offaly, was the largest in the world from 1845 to 1915. His son Charles Parsons invented the steam turbine in 1884. It was first demonstrated in his vessel *Turbinia* for Queen Victoria's diamond jubilee in 1897 and established a new world water-speed record. Charles's brother Laurence was first to estimate the temperature of the surface of the moon.

The first scientist to discover why the sky is blue was John Tyndall from County Carlow in 1859.

George Francis Fitzgerald, one of Ireland's leading scientists, constructed a glider in 1895 and tested it in the grounds of Trinity College Dublin. It flew well without a passenger but would only carry Fitzgerald a few yards.